The Oil Industry

Development or DESTRUCTION?

The Oil Industry

Richard Spilsbury and Louise Spilsbury

rosen publishing's
rosen central

NEW YORK

**Library of Congress
Cataloging-in-Publication Data**

Spilsbury, Richard, 1963–
The oil industry/Richard Spilsbury, Louise Spilsbury.—1st ed.
    p. cm.—(Development or destruction?)
Includes bibliographical references and index.
ISBN 978-1-4488-6991-6 (library binding)—
ISBN 978-1-4488-6998-5 (pbk.)—
ISBN 978-1-4488-6999-2 (6-pack)
1. Petroleum industry and trade—Juvenile literature. I. Spilsbury, Louise. II. Title.
HD9560.5.S65 2012
338.2'7282—dc23

2011033317

Manufactured in the United States of America

CPSIA Compliance Information: Batch #W12YA: For further information, contact Rosen Publishing, New York, New York, at 1-800-237-9932.

Picture acknowledgments:

The author and publisher would like to thank the following agencies for allowing these pictures to be reproduced: Alamy/Christine Osborne Pictures:
p14; Alamy/Friedrich Stark: p23; Alamy/WoodyStock: p28; Alamy/AlamyCelebrity: pp40–41; Corbis/Ed Kashi: p22, p24; Corbis/Thomas Ashby/
Reuters: p25; Corbis/George Steinmetz: p26, p35; Corbis/Natalie Fobes/Science Faction: p36; Getty/Arnulf Husmo: front cover, p29; Getty: p3, p18
(top), p13 (top); Getty/Bloomberg: p16, p18 (bottom); Getty/AFP: p19; Getty/National Geographic: p21; iStock: p4, p5, p8, p13 (bottom), p38;
ESA: p24; Rex/Actionpress: p32; Sciencephoto/Dr Davidhall: p42; Shutterstock: p5, p9, p11, p12, p14, p17, p20, pp36–37, p43; Statoil: all images
pp30–31; All locator maps: Shutterstock.

Images used throughout for creative graphics: iStockphoto, Shutterstock.
Should there be any inadvertent omission, please apply to the publisher for rectification.

Contents

The importance of oil

Oil has made a bigger impact on our world in the last 100 years than any other natural resource. It is the major fuel for vehicles, allowing the transport of goods and people globally. It is also a vital raw material for many industries. The use and trade of oil has had a major influence on the economic development of countries around the world. Oil has often been called black gold – because crude oil taken from the ground is thick and black and because oil is such a valuable commodity.

△ Oil fuels the global fleet of airplanes, trucks, cars, motorcycles, and ships.

Uses of oil

Crude oil contains a mix of different useful substances that are extracted in industrial plants, called oil refineries. About 60 percent of all crude oil is refined into petroleum fuels, which are burned in engines to power anything from cars to chainsaws. Other refined products include asphalt, important for surfacing roads, and petrochemicals. For example, the petrochemical ethylene is used to make the common plastic polyethylene, PVC, and also polyester, which is used in fabrics. Other petrochemicals are made into a wide range of products including polystyrene, rubber, dyes, paints, fertilizers, bulletproof vests, and even some medicines, such as aspirin.

Where oil is found

Oil is not distributed evenly around the world, as it's only found in certain types of rocks. Areas of rock where oil is found in large quantities that can be accessed by people are called oil reserves. More than half of the

North America

South America

world's crude oil reserves are found in the Middle East, and Saudi Arabia has the largest oil reserves of any country — about 20 percent of the world's total. The other main oil reserves are found in Canada, the US, Latin America, Africa, and Russia.

Who owns oil reserves?

In general, oil reserves are owned by the country on whose territory they are found. Oil is extremely valuable and countries with large reserves are often rich. Usually countries divide up their land and ocean areas where there might be oil into portions called concessions. Oil companies with skills and expertise in finding and extracting oil pay for licences to explore particular concessions. The companies sell the oil they produce on a concession and pay taxes to the country on the amount they extract. Oil companies may be wholly owned by countries, such as Saudi Aramco of Saudi Arabia, or privately owned, such as BP and ExxonMobil.

Europe

Asia

Africa

The blue areas on this world map show oil fields that have been discovered to date.

Australasia

Antarctica

Oil formation and extraction

Oil is a nonrenewable energy resource. It formed from the remains of microscopic ocean plants and animals that died millions of years ago. They were buried in layers of sand and mud at the bottom of ancient seas. Over time the layers turned into sedimentary rock deep underground. High pressure and heat there gradually turned the remains into drops of crude oil. The drops mostly collected in spaces or cracks within rocks or in larger gaps between rock layers.

Reserves may be below the land surface (onshore) or under the sea bed (offshore). In order to reach onshore oil reserves, oil companies drill deep wells through or along rock layers. Offshore oil companies drill from oil platforms (or rigs) built on stilts or floating on the sea surface. In order to retrieve the oil, platforms use pipes called risers. High pressure underground often forces oil out of the rock to the surface. If there isn't enough pressure, liquids are injected into the reserves or pumps are used to suck out the oil. Some oil is found at the surface, soaked into soft rocks called oil shale and tar sands. These are mined, crushed, and heated to release the oil inside them. Once oil has been extracted, it is usually transported to an oil refinery across land by long-distance pipes or by sea on massive ships called tankers.

⌃ **Oil drilling is much safer than it was in the past, but there is still a risk that oil will catch fire, and high underground pressure can blow out drills and underground pipes.**

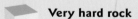

■ Very hard rock

□ Porous rock containing gas

■ Porous rock containing oil

■ Porous rock containing water

⌃ **Onshore wells need to drill through at least one layer of very hard rock to access oil reserves.**

8

Destruction fact

Two pints (.94 liters) of oil is enough to pollute 1,900,000 pints (900,000 liters) of drinking water.

The downside of oil

Burning oil-based fuels to release energy also releases waste gases. Carbon dioxide collects in the atmosphere, stores heat, and most scientists believe it contributes to climate change. Other gases cause air pollution, affecting human health. The extraction and transport of oil may also damage the environment. Accidents as well as regular oil company activities cause water and land pollution. These impacts and the uneven distribution of oil profits cause conflicts.

Do the benefits of oil production balance out destruction of these sorts? And are there more sustainable solutions, lessening the impact of the oil industry? This book considers this question by examining five international case studies.

▽ Oil exploration and production bring benefits and problems all over the world. The five case studies in this book look at some of the major issues and impacts today.

How did Norway make sure North Sea oil discoveries benefitted its people? (pages 28–33).

What effects will the race for oil from the Lomonosov Ridge and other parts of the Arctic Ocean have on this remote region? (pages 34–39).

The Deepwater Horizon oil spill alerted the world to the risks of deep drilling. How has it impacted the Gulf of Mexico oil industry? (pages 16–21).

Find out how the discovery and exploitation of oil riches in the Niger Delta have created great environmental and social problems. (pages 22–27).

Oil wealth from fields such as Zakum transformed Abu Dhabi, but can development continue? (pages 10–15).

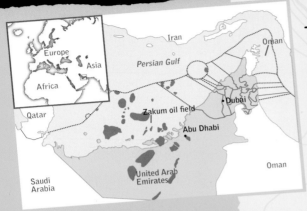

The United Arab Emirates (UAE) in the Middle East is a country about the size of Iceland that edges on the Persian Gulf. It is made up of seven states, or emirates, the largest of which is Abu Dhabi. It is also the richest emirate, mainly because it controls the country's biggest oil field – Zakum.

△ This map shows the oil fields that have been discovered in the UAE. The dotted lines mark the concession borders.

Oil exports

Around two-thirds of the world's crude oil reserves are located in the countries bordering the Persian Gulf. The oil is exported by fleets of oil tankers and pipelines to countries around the world, such as China and India. The pie chart below shows the share of oil produced by different Gulf countries.

A brief history of Middle East oil

Oil had been used in small quantities in the Middle East for millennia, for example for lamps, but at the start of the twentieth century oil was increasingly in demand. Major world powers such as Britain, Germany, and the US needed oil-based fuel, especially for their fleets of military ships. Britain, France, and Germany had long had political influence over and even controlled parts of the Middle East because of its ideal position for trade with Asia and Africa. Therefore, their oil companies, including Anglo-Persian Oil, which later became BP, explored for oil in concessions across the region.

The first major oil discovery in the Middle East was made in Iran in 1908. During the following decades, oil was found throughout the Persian Gulf region, including Abu Dhabi in 1953. Global demand for oil grew because of the increasing use of cars and aircraft, and the large reserves of the Middle East, especially Saudi Arabia, could meet that demand. Today the Middle East produces more oil than any other region in the world.

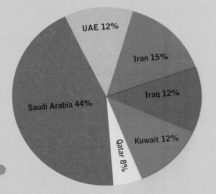

UAE 12%
Iran 15%
Iraq 12%
Saudi Arabia 44%
Kuwait 12%
Qatar 8%

Chapter 2

ON THE SCENE

"Beneath the glistening waters off the coast of Abu Dhabi lies one of the world's largest oil fields...an estimated 50 billion barrels of oil sit below the sea."

Morten Mauritzen, ExxonMobil, Abu Dhabi, 2010

The Zakum oil field

In 1955 the ruler of Abu Dhabi sold exploration rights for offshore Abu Dhabi to the Abu Dhabi Marine Areas (ADMA) company, owned by the foreign oil companies BP and Total. Their geologists drilled into the seafloor from ships in order to get rock samples and check them for oil content. Some oil was found in 1958, but the giant Zakum reserve was discovered in 1963. Over the next four years, BP and Total built platforms to drill for Zakum oil. They installed pipelines taking the oil to nearby Zirku Island and built a port there so that tankers could collect the oil.

The Abu Dhabi government got 50 percent of ADMA profits on oil sales. In 1971 the government set up the Abu Dhabi National Oil Company to take more control, and profit more, from oil produced on its territory. It bought part of ADMA and its oil infrastructure. The government also worked in partnership with other oil companies to produce more oil from different parts of Zakum. Today there are tens of platforms and hundreds of wells, which, together with the other infrastructure, form the enormous Zakum oil field – the fourth largest oil field in the world.

Vital statistics:

Zakum oil field

Location: 50 miles (80 km) offshore
Area: 1,500 km² (560 square miles)
Depth of oil: 1.5 miles (2.4 km) beneath the seafloor
Depth of Persian Gulf: up to 85 feet (26 m)
Number of wells: over 500
Current production: over 790,000 barrels of oil per day – enough to fill 45 Olympic swimming pools

Oil sales make up nearly half the value of Abu Dhabi exports and contribute to a GDP of $160 billion. Dividing up Abu Dhabi's wealth between all its citizens would give them $90,000 each per year!

The oil wealth of Abu Dhabi has paid for the development of a high standard of living for its citizens and access to a luxury lifestyle.

Transformation of a city-state

Abu Dhabi is both the capital city and an emirate of the UAE. Until the 1950s, the major industry in the small island town of Abu Dhabi was pearl fishing and there were no paved roads in the UAE. Abu Dhabi developed from the 1970s onward because the government was earning increasing oil revenue from oil companies operating wells in its concessions. The government spent a large amount of the revenue on improving infrastructure both for the oil industry and for Abu Dhabi citizens. It invested in a network of roads linking the city with onshore oil fields, and installed running water, a sewerage system, and electrical supply to households. It also built schools and government buildings.

Today Abu Dhabi is the richest city in the world. It has many modern high-rise buildings, international hotels, multilane highways, and luxury shopping malls. Abu Dhabi's population of around 650,000 is seven times larger than in 1975, partly because of migrant workers in the oil industry. International influences have caused some cultural change. For example, in the past, it was not acceptable for women to work in the UAE. Today women make up over 60 percent of the workforce in state jobs such as in government and teaching.

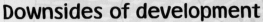

Downsides of development

Drilling and transporting oil always causes some oil spills. Some are accidental while others are caused by washing out tankers. Because of the high volume of oil tanker traffic around Abu Dhabi, 1 million barrels of oil are spilled each year. Spilled oil and other chemicals used by the oil industry can poison or choke many marine organisms and damage plants such as seagrass, which are important wildlife habitats. Dredging the seabed to deepen channels for boats also destroys seagrass. Populations of dugongs are dwindling, partly because they do not have enough seagrass to eat.

Oil has made most UAE citizens rich. They rarely take on the low-paid jobs in oil or construction industries. Around 95 percent of such jobs are carried out by migrant workers from Asian countries such as Nepal and India. They can earn more in the UAE than they can at home, but they are exploited by working long hours for low wages that are often not paid for months on end. Rents are so high in the city that migrant workers usually live in poor housing.

Migrant workers in Abu Dhabi who have contributed to its economic development are sometimes forced to live in hostel rooms with up to 20 other people.

EXPLORE FURTHER

Find out how the neighboring UAE Dubai became rich even though it has little oil. Why did the global financial crisis affect its growth?

Dugongs were once hunted but are now officially protected by the Abu Dhabi government. However, they are threatened by the environmental impact of oil development.

Abu Dhabi investments

Abu Dhabi's future success relies in part on continuing oil and also gas revenues from Zakum. However, it is costly to get oil from Zakum due to the low pressure of oil in parts of the field and the high cost of drilling new wells or extending existing ones to reach it. This is why Abu Dhabi is also investing in oil and gas developments in other parts of the world such as Indonesia, Thailand, and Canada, as well as in non-oil industries overseas. These industries range from part ownership of Gatwick Airport in the UK to mines in Africa.

▲ The Abu Dhabi government has invested some of its oil wealth in properties worldwide, including an estimated $800 million in 2008 to buy the famous Chrysler Building in New York.

Artificial islands

The World Islands off the coast of Dubai are formed by sand dredged from the floor of the Gulf. To complete the formation of these islands 390 million cubic yards (300 million cubic m) of sand will have to be deposited in an area where the seabed is between 11 and 18 yards (10 and 17 m). The sand needed for the project is dredged from the open sea. Each island will be up to above sea level. The main contractors for the World Islands are Van Oord ACZ Marine Contractors Gulf FZE – Dubai, which are responsible for land reclamation, dredging works, and the breakwaters. This is the largest project Van Oord has undertaken in the region.

▲ A ship sprays out sand mined from the open sea to create an artificial island in shallow Persian Gulf waters.

Zakum oil field, Abu Dhabi (UAE)

Individuals, banks, and other organizations in Abu Dhabi are also investing in a range of industries to create work and revenue, so the emirate is not completely dependent on oil. These include the largest aluminium processing facility in the world and Saadiyat Island, an artificial island built for tourism. It will be home to world-class museums, such as a new Louvre. A further project is Masdar, a sustainable city. This is a revolutionary, solar-powered settlement for 50,000 people on the outskirts of Abu Dhabi city. It includes electric cars, and is planned for completion by 2025. However, Abu Dhabi citizens are some of the highest users of energy in the world, from electricity to power air conditioning, to fuel for their gas-guzzling cars. Reducing Abu Dhabi's energy consumption would have a bigger impact on climate change than building Masdar.

Development or Destruction?

Development:

* Abu Dhabi's Zakum oil field has contributed to making the UAE the 7th biggest exporter of oil in the world.
* Abu Dhabi offers a high standard of living for its citizens.
* The emirate is using its oil wealth to diversify industry and to invest in sustainable energy use, ready for a future when less oil will be available.

Destruction:

* Oil development in Abu Dhabi has caused coastal pollution and environmental damage.
* Abu Dhabi citizens have among the largest carbon footprints in the world.
* Oil wealth has created higher living standards for Abu Dhabi citizens, but some of its migrant workers face social injustice.

Oil has been vital to the development of the US as a whole, as well as to particular regions, such as the Gulf of Mexico. In 2010, the industry there changed overnight following a catastrophic accident on a single rig. This highlighted the dangers of offshore drilling.

Development fact

Cheap oil from Spindletop spurred the Texan Santa Fe railway to change fuel from coal to the more efficient oil. There was one oil-driven locomotive in 1901, but 250 by 1905.

US oil development

Individuals and their small companies first drilled for oil in the US in the mid- to late nineteenth century. Back then oil was mostly refined to make kerosene for burning in lamps, but little else. In spring 1901, enormous quantities of oil were found in Texas, in a location called Spindletop. By the end of the year there were 200 wells operated by 100 private companies at Spindletop. Some of these turned into the major oil companies of today, including Gulf Oil.

▽ There are thousands of oil rigs dotting the coastal waters of the Gulf of Mexico.

Oil states took taxes from oil companies based on how much oil was found, but there was no law preventing companies claiming public land where they found oil as their own until 1920.

Up to the 1940s the major oil-producing states were Texas and California. However, as onshore reserves dwindled, oil companies focused on searching for offshore oil in the Gulf of Mexico.

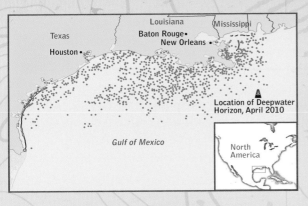

Louisiana
Mississippi
Texas
Baton Rouge
New Orleans
Houston

Location of Deepwater
Horizon, April 2010

Gulf of Mexico

North
America

△ **Rigs off the Gulf of Mexico (indicated by red dots on this map) are mostly located in the shallowest water where reserves are easiest to exploit. However, the largest, most lucrative new reserves are in deeper parts, farther out to sea.**

Into the Gulf

Gulf of Mexico oil was first found seeping from the marshes of Louisiana. Oil companies brought in experienced oil workers from Texas to find oil reserves and employed locals who knew how to find their way through the dense marshes. The companies built piers from solid land to drill from the marshes, and in 1911 Gulf Oil created the first offshore rig to drill under a lake. In the 1940s to '50s, oil rigs gradually spread from the coastal edge farther out into the deeper water in the Gulf, because geologists had located large reserves of high-pressure oil there. By then, oil companies had developed rigs that could remain stable in deep water, drill down into the seabed for many miles, and survive strong waves and storms.

By 2010 there were around 4,000 rigs in the Gulf of Mexico, one of which was the *Deepwater Horizon*. This was a floating rig with motors that could move it to different parts of the Gulf to drill. Using a floating rig is cheaper and causes less seafloor damage than setting up a fixed rig.

Vital statistics:

Deepwater Horizon

Built: 2001
Owner: Transocean, Ltd., a specialist offshore drilling company
Length: 374 feet (114 m) – the length of a big football pitch
Height: 134 feet (41 m)
Weight: 35,825 (32,500 tonnes)
Record: Drilled deepest well in history at 6.6 miles (10.6 km)

Chapter 3

17

Blowout

From February 2010, *Deepwater Horizon* had been rented by the oil company BP. On the night of April 20, 2010, the crew on the rig had just spent weeks drilling down over 3 miles (5 km) into a possible oil-producing reserve called Macondo. They had sealed the drill hole with mud and concrete until BP was ready to collect the oil. But then a surge of gas and oil broke through the seal and shot up the riser. The blowout set the rig on fire, killing and injuring workers, and it sank. With no seal, up to 60,000 barrels of oil poured out of the hole each day.

BP used submarine robots to lower a heavy dome over the hole to stop the leak, but gas emerging from the drill hole floated it off. It put a giant steel funnel over the hole, attached to a pipe that took some oil up to a waiting tanker. Eventually, in September it managed to drill another hole and forced concrete into the Macondo well to plug it. By then, 5 million barrels of oil had spilled into the Gulf of Mexico – enough to fill nearly 300 Olympic swimming pools.

▷ **Fireboats battle to stop the ferocious flames on the remaining section of the *Deepwater Horizon*, shortly before it sank.**

Innovations: Blowout preventers

Blowout preventers (BOPs) are special heavy valves placed over oil wells. They have hydraulic rams that automatically cut through and shut off the riser when high-pressure oil moves through it. This should prevent a blowout. However, the BOP on the Macondo well failed, possibly because the hydraulics did not work.

◁ **A blowout preventer similar to the one that failed on *Deepwater*'s Macondo well.**

Environmental impacts

The oil spill from *Deepwater Horizon*'s well formed a vast floating slick that gradually moved toward the shores of Louisiana and adjoining states. Sticky crude oil coated many coastal shores, killing plants and sea life, such as crabs and oysters, and blackened beaches. Thousands of oil-soaked animals including pelicans and sea turtles could not move or feed, and many died as a result.

A response team organized by the US government and partly funded by BP cleaned up the oil. They dug tar from beaches and rescued oiled animals. Wildlife rescue experts carefully used detergent to clean off oil, fed the animals, and released them back into the wild. They skimmed oil from the water surface using booms dragged by boats. They also sprayed chemicals called dispersants on the slick. These broke the oil up into small pieces that sank before more oil reached the coasts. However, tiny young of fish such as tuna or shrimp that breed in the Gulf may die when they accidentally eat the oil pieces. This could impact on the future stocks of these economically important fish.

⋁ **Volunteers clean an oil-covered brown pelican, affected by the BP *Deepwater Horizon* oil spill in the Gulf of Mexico, found off the Louisiana coast.**

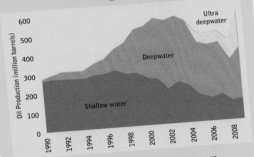

Going deeper

Oil Production (million barrel(s))

Ultra deepwater

Deepwater

Shallow water

600
500
400
300
200
100
0

1990 1992 1994 1996 1998 2000 2002 2004 2006 2008

The Gulf of Mexico oil industry is important to the US – it supplies one-third of US domestic oil. This graph reveals that every year since the 1990s, more oil in the Gulf of Mexico has come from wells in deeper water. The reason is that supplies from wells closer to land are dwindling, yet US and global demand for oil is growing.

▽ The Baton Rouge oil refinery has developed from its first beginnings in 1909 to become the second largest in the US, employing around 6,000 people.

The Louisiana economy

Gulf of Mexico oil changed the Louisiana economy in the mid-twentieth century. It created employment on rigs, boats supplying rigs, and in refineries. The oil supplied raw materials for petrochemical factories. Oil revenue was used to drain the marshes to create coastal land for settlements and farming. It has funded state schools and public services, and the growth of big regional cities such as Baton Rouge, home to many oil companies. However, oil wealth does not benefit all Louisiana's citizens. The state has some of the highest proportions of people unemployed or living in poverty in the US. One reason for this is that since the late 1980s there have been fewer low-skill jobs available.

The *Deepwater Horizon* disaster put a further strain on the economy. President Obama suspended all deep drilling in the Gulf for six months afterward owing to concerns about the safety of wells. Thousands of Louisiana citizens became temporarily unemployed because a third of jobs in coastal Louisiana are in the oil industry.

Unloading pink shrimp from the depths of the Gulf of Mexico on a trawler.

Recovery?

Fishing and shrimping were suspended in a third of the Gulf's waters because of possible oil contamination of seafood. Tourists were kept away from coastal resorts owing to tar-stained sands and the smell of oil in the air. Many affected individuals and businesses were helped out by compensation payments from BP and by an injection of government money. By 2011, beaches were mostly clean and fishing and oil exploration had resumed. However, scientists have found a thick layer of oil on the seafloor in deep waters. This could have long-term pollution impacts for the Gulf of Mexico.

Development or Destruction?

Development:

* Oil has created employment and development in Louisiana and other Gulf of Mexico states.
* The Macondo well blowout happened because of equipment failure, but other deep wells are producing oil safely.
* Gulf of Mexico oil is essential for the US economy as a whole.

Destruction:

* The Deepwater Horizon disaster killed people and wildlife, and caused unemployment in the region.
* BP's response to the disaster was too slow, allowing too much oil to spill.
* The long-term pollution of the Gulf could impact fishing and the food industry for years to come.

Niger Delta, Nigeria

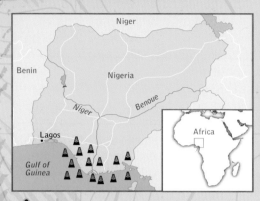

Nigeria's oil fields and industry are concentrated in the southeast of the country.

Nigeria is an oil-rich country, yet the majority of its people live in poverty. Most of its oil comes from the highly populated Niger Delta, where impacts of the industry such as pollution cause conflict.

Oil development

In the early twentieth century Nigeria was part of the British Empire and Britain controlled its resources, including oil. In 1938, the British government sold licenses to explore concessions covering the whole country to oil company Shell D'Arcy. Shell, as it was later known, made its first large oil discovery under the Delta region of the Niger River in 1956. Two years later, it sold on licenses for some concessions to other oil companies, including Mobil and Agip, in order to concentrate its resources on building wells and pipelines in the Delta oil fields. Nigeria became independent from Britain in 1960, but the foreign companies continued to control the oil exploration and production.

A woman in a fishing village of the Niger Delta, overshadowed by the oil industry infrastructure.

Chapter 4

Destruction fact

Drilling for oil in the Niger Delta releases lots of natural gas from underground. This is wasted and burned off, as there is so little demand.

Following a civil war in the Delta region in the late 1960s, the Nigerian military government increased state participation in the oil industry to earn more money from oil than just concession rents. It took stakes in the foreign oil companies, so it earned a share of each company's profits in return for letting the companies continue to operate in the country. The 1970s Nigerian oil exploration and production rose because its oil was cheaper than that from many other regions, and it was in demand from the US. Today Nigeria supplies 40 percent of US oil. The Nigerian government used some of its oil revenue to build transport infrastructure.

Pollution in the oil fields

People in the Niger Delta oil fields live in a heavily polluted environment. Oil seeps from old, unused pipes and is spilled along with toxic chemicals from refineries, wells, or tankers. Spills are an enormous problem. A report by Amnesty International claimed that nearly twice the amount of oil lost by *Deepwater Horizon* (see page 18) is spilled in Nigeria each year. The oil pollutes farmland, making crops unsafe to eat, and also contaminates water, killing fish and making it unsafe to drink.

In 2004 scientists sampled water from around the Delta and found it contained around five times the safe limit of cancer-causing toxins that is recommended by the World Health Organization. Burning waste gas from the oil industry in Nigeria releases toxic gases and particles, which cause breathing problems and create more greenhouse gases than the rest of Africa south of the Sahara.

A boy stands in an oil-contaminated area in Ogoniland, Nigeria.

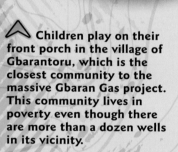

Children play on their front porch in the village of Gbarantoru, which is the closest community to the massive Gbaran Gas project. This community lives in poverty even though there are more than a dozen wells in its vicinity.

Poverty in Nigeria

Today Nigeria oil exports are worth around $70 billion per year. Nevertheless, two-thirds of Nigerians live in poverty. This is partly because of the Nigerian government.

Some people claim that corrupt generals running the government, especially in the 1980s and '90s, stole hundreds of billions of dollars of oil revenue. In this period the government invested little in its country, so today there is inadequate health care and less than half of Nigerians have access to clean water and electricity. Although there is officially low unemployment in the country, few people can get well-paid jobs – the average income for a Nigerian citizen is the same as it was in 1960. Better-paid oil industry jobs in the Niger Delta are mostly taken by foreign oil workers or people from particular Nigerian tribes with government influence.

Problems are made worse by dependency on oil. By the 1980s, revenue from oil overtook that from former major export crops like palm oil and peanuts. Farming declined because many Nigerians migrated to expanding cities, such as Lagos, in the hope of finding better-paid work.

Vital statistics:

Nigeria

Population: 160 million
Export earnings: 95 percent from oil
Below poverty line: 66 percent
Life expectancy in Niger Delta: 40 years
Health spending per person: $2
(UN recommends $34)

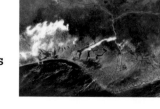

Niger Delta, Nigeria

Subsistence farmers in the polluted Delta lands struggled to grow enough food for their families. With less farming, there was not enough food to feed the growing population. The Nigerian government has had to use oil revenue to import staple foods ever since.

Conflict and violence

During the 1980s ethnic groups including the Ogoni people in the Niger Delta began peaceful protests. These were directed at Shell, which produces half of Nigeria's oil, and the Nigerian government. They protested against pollution and the violence used to move villagers off their land to allow oil exploration. They also protested against poverty and unemployment in an oil-rich region. In 1996, for example, Shell employed just 88 Ogoni in their Delta operations – around 2 percent of the workforce. Thousands of protestors occupied and forced closure of Shell facilities.

At the time, Shell and other oil companies had great influence on the Nigerian government, as the oil industry created such revenue for the country. The companies encouraged the government to stop protests. For example, Shell supplied weapons and paid for military missions against particular villages where protest leaders came from, while Chevron used its helicopters to bring in navy personnel who shot protesting youths. The Ogoni struggle became known internationally, following the trial and execution by the government of the popular Ogoni environmental leader Ken Saro-Wiwa in 1995. Government forces murdered over 2,000 protestors and destroyed whole villages. Locals fought back and bombed oil pipelines and kidnapped oil workers.

◁ **Militia groups in the Niger Delta region say that they are fighting for a fair share of the oil wealth. However, the Nigerian government and oil companies claim that these groups are trying to claim river routes that are used by oil smugglers to export stolen crude oil.**

Destruction fact

Nigeria's few oil refineries are badly maintained and inefficient, so the government of this oil-rich country imports refined fuels from as far away as Europe. This transportation causes huge environmental damage.

Changes in Nigeria

Since 2008 the Nigerian government has tried to stop violence in the Niger Delta. For example, it has offered money to armed militants to stop fighting and disrupting oil production, and has offered a percentage of regional oil revenue to local tribes. In 2010 President Jonathan announced that the government would use oil revenue to make improvements in power supply and in the roads of Nigeria for the benefit of all Nigerians. However, the problems of pollution and poverty in Nigeria will take a long time to be rectified.

Learning from mistakes

The story of the impact of the oil industry in many African countries is similar to that in Nigeria. For example Lusaka, the capital of Angola, developed rapidly using oil revenue and foreign investment from countries such as China that import their oil, but remains totally dependent on oil exports.

In an almost daily routine, cars line up for gas in Port Harcourt, Nigeria. Many of Nigeria's petroleum refineries are no longer functioning, as corrupt government officials find it more lucrative to export crude oil and import refined fuels from neighboring countries.

EXPLORE FURTHER

Find out how Malaysia used its oil revenue from the 1970s onward to develop different industries. What are its biggest exports today?

People living in oil-producing areas are in conflict with government forces over land and gain little benefit from oil. The government of Ghana, which discovered oil in 2010, hopes to learn from these mistakes. For example, it plans to invest some oil revenue in a range of industries, including the cocoa industry and aluminium production, as well as in health, education, and other basic needs. It also wants to work with foreign oil companies to extract oil while providing Ghanaians with oil industry jobs.

Development or Destruction?

Development:

* Oil from the Niger Delta increased Nigeria's GDP, funded development, and made some Nigerians rich.
* Oil provides almost all of Nigeria's export revenue.
* In the twenty-first century Nigerian politicians are trying to share the benefits of oil more fairly, especially in the Delta region.

Destruction:

* Oil development has created ongoing conflict between people living on oil-rich land, the government, and foreign oil companies, killing thousands of people.
* Oil development has caused environmental destruction in the Delta, which has impacted on people's health and jobs.
* Oil revenue has benefitted only some Nigerians, while many live in worse poverty than 40 years ago.

Norway, like Nigeria, discovered large reserves of oil in the late 1950s, yet while only few profit from oil revenue in Nigeria, the opposite is the case in Norway. The reason is that the Norwegian government, and the state oil company Statoil in particular, used oil revenue to carefully develop and sustain the industry.

▲ Western Europe's largest oil and gas reserves are under the North Sea. Norway controls about 57 percent of them. This map shows both the oil reserves and pipelines (in blue) and the gas reserves and pipelines (in pink). Concession borders are in orange.

North Sea oil

In 1959 the Netherlands found a gas and oil field near Groningen that extended under the North Sea. This began a race by countries around the North Sea to discover their own offshore oil supplies. At first exploration was on parts of the continental shelf off Germany and Denmark, where drilling was easiest. Then its exploration moved farther offshore into Norwegian and British waters. After years of expensive, largely unsuccessful test drilling in the late 1960s, oil companies were about to give up exploration.

But in December 1969, the Ocean Viking rig, operated by Phillips Petroleum on behalf of Norwegian oil company Norsk Hydro, discovered large amounts of oil 1.9 miles (3 km) beneath the seafloor in the Ekofisk field. Ekofisk started producing oil in 1971 and Norway made many more major oil and gas discoveries over the next two decades. The UK started production from its own offshore oil fields in 1975. In 2011 there were over 300 oil and gas fields in the North Sea, spreading from north of the Shetlands, Scotland, to around 499 miles (640 km) farther south.

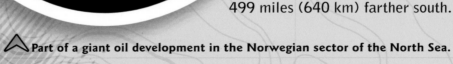

▲ Part of a giant oil development in the Norwegian sector of the North Sea.

Chapter 5

Development fact

From the 1970s onward Stavanger grew from a small fishing town to Norway's oil capital. The population almost tripled and it has the nation's highest proportion of oil workers.

Taking control of oil

The Norwegian government realized that the North Sea could provide enormous amounts of revenue, so in 1972 it established a state oil company, Statoil, to develop Norwegian oil resources. It also set up the Norwegian Petroleum Directorate (NPD) to regulate how the oil companies, including Statoil, worked together and how the country spent oil revenue. For example, NPD decided to invest in non-oil industries providing long-term work. It created a welfare fund for Norwegians, as well as investing in technology to help preserve the environment when exploiting the oil. Unlike Nigeria, Norway invested in developing oil fields, using the technical skills of foreign oil companies such as Phillips, while also strongly regulating the industry. This prevented any one company or interest group from gaining too much power over Norwegian oil.

▽ **Gullfaks C oil platform being constructed in a Norwegian yard before being installed in the North Sea for operation.**

Statoil

Statoil grew following discovery of the major fields Statfjord and Gullfaks in the 1970s. Today Statoil controls around 80 percent of Norway's oil and gas production. It has become a world leader in finding oil, aided by Norwegian investment in oil technology research at universities. Statoil has particular expertise in technology that helps extract oil from deep offshore fields. For example, it has developed units resting on the seafloor that can drill into oil fields and also create links into existing subsea pipelines.

Statoil uses robot submarines equipped with cameras and pressure sensors to operate this technology, controlled from computers on ships. It is much cheaper and less damaging to the seafloor to do this than to drill in deep water from surface rigs or lay new pipelines.

Oil drilling and production aided by robots reduce risks to personnel and costs.

Statoil uses cutting-edge computer technology to create high-resolution images of oil fields that can be used to improve drilling efficiency.

Innovations: Recovering more oil

When oil fields start to empty, oil companies try to extract or recover more oil from the rock in different ways. Statoil forces in gas and seawater to flush out oil and also injects bacteria to help extract the oil. It has automated systems that separate oil coming out of wells from water and sand at the bottom of the sea. Statoil has also developed sophisticated 3-D computer images of oil fields so that it knows exactly where to drill to find the most oil.

Oil and GDP

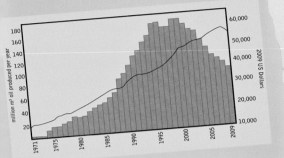

Norway and UK oil

Norway produces over half of all North Sea oil. Since the first oil discovery it has developed wells, refineries, and other oil assets worth more than $98 billion. Around one-tenth of government revenue comes from offshore oil and gas, and a quarter of a million people work in its oil industry. The UK produces far less oil, even though its fields are larger than Norway's, and UK citizens have benefitted less from oil revenue. This is partly because the UK government gave more control of oil production to independent companies, which reduced revenue. It also did not invest so much revenue in developing other UK industries.

In order to find out whether oil industry development in a country is sustainable, it is important to look at data that will reveal whether the economy of a country is entirely dependent on the oil industry. This chart shows two things. The bar chart shows how North Sea oil production in Norway grew from the 1960s and peaked in 2001. Since then production has fallen, as reserves have started to run out. The line graph shows Norway's GDP – a measure of the wealth of a country divided by its number of citizens. Norway's GDP has continued to grow even when oil production has fallen. This means that Norwegian economic success is not entirely due to producing oil, but also relies on other industries.

The refinery at Mongstad has a capacity of 11 million tons of crude oil a year. The refinery is the largest in Norway and is part-owned by Statoil.

Existing oil infrastructure

Oil and gas rigs and wells often only last for around 50 or 60 years in the North Sea, either because oil fields dry up or the structure weakens in the rough conditions. The NPD is concerned that some older, less productive Statoil wells, such as those in the Gullfaks field, were not maintained properly and could be at risk of leaks or blowouts. However, it is very expensive to close up deep wells and it is often cheaper to sink old rigs into deep water than to dismantle them. This is a very controversial solution because residual oil and chemicals in the structures can cause ocean pollution. Statoil has many old rigs and faces some difficult decisions in the future about their disposal.

Greenpeace demonstrators occupying Brent Spar oil rig to prevent Shell disposing of the rig in the sea.

Destruction fact

Experts estimate that 40 percent of the 500 offshore North Sea installations may need to be taken down and disposed of by the companies that built them in the next 20 to 30 years.

New frontiers

Norway's North Sea oil reserves are gradually decreasing, so it is searching for oil in deeper, more northerly regions. For example, in 2013 Statoil plans to start producing oil from the new Goliat field in the Barents Sea. Such Arctic exploration is very controversial, owing to pollution concerns (see page 36). The Norwegian government is also investing in the oil industry worldwide under the Oil for Development program. This aims to help less economically developed countries with oil reserves to manage their oil resources in a sustainable way. Some people question whether the program has been right to support the oil industry in places such as Nigeria where the industry has had severe negative impacts (see page 24).

Development or Destruction?

Development:

* Norway has used North Sea oil revenue to benefit its citizens through careful development of its state-run oil industry, Statoil.
* Statoil uses up-to-date technology to produce oil efficiently.
* Statoil shares its expertise worldwide with poorer countries. The environmental impact of oil production is carefully regulated in Norway.

Destruction:

* North Sea oil is running out, and when Statoil invests in other countries, it may have less control over production and revenue.
* Statoil has collaborated with countries such as Nigeria where most local people benefit little from oil revenue.
* Statoil is investing elsewhere when it has North Sea wells and platforms that need maintenance or disposal.

How much oil in the Arctic?

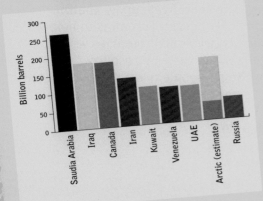

The Lomonosov Ridge is a mountain range at the bottom of the Arctic Ocean. It runs underneath the North Pole and the rest of the Arctic ice cap. Countries bordering the ocean are claiming ownership of this ridge because there may be enormous oil reserves beneath it. They need this oil for development and revenue, yet the Arctic oil rush has the potential to harm the fragile environment of the Arctic Ocean.

The bar chart above shows the major proven reserves of oil remaining worldwide. It also shows the estimate of Arctic oil. This refers to a 2009 US Geological Survey report based on oil found in the samples of rock drilled from around the region – both onshore and offshore – and the knowledge of where similar rocks are found. There is uncertainty about the exact amount of oil, so the estimate is a range of values.

The disputed Lomonosov Ridge is under deep polar water between Russia, the US, Canada, and Greenland. In the winter, this part of the Arctic Ocean is frozen over.

Russian claims

Russia does not have the biggest oil reserves, yet is the world's biggest producer of crude oil, largely from oil fields in western Siberia. However, its onshore fields are running out because of high production of oil for both domestic use and export.

▽ A drilling ship in the pack ice of the Arctic Ocean carrying out a test drill to see whether underwater rocks contain oil. The guard is keeping a lookout for polar bears!

Chapter 6

ON THE SCENE

"It's a very important move for Russia to demonstrate its potential in the Arctic. It's like putting a flag on the Moon."

Sergei Balyasnikov, Russian Arctic and Antarctic Institute, 2007

Therefore, the country is increasingly searching for oil in Russian sectors of the Arctic Ocean. Normally coastal countries can exploit subsea resources for up to 200 miles (322 km) away from their coasts. But Russian scientists had test-drilled the seafloor farther out than this and found it potentially held large amounts of oil.

In 2007 a Russian submarine containing a small team of explorers voyaged to the Lomonosov Ridge and planted a Russian flag on it! This was to symbolically claim ownership of the Ridge and an area of surrounding seafloor, totalling the size of western Europe. The Russians claimed they could do this because the Ridge is an underwater extension of Russian Arctic lands. Controlling this area would potentially double Russian oil reserves as the scientists estimated there were up to 75 billion barrels of oil beneath the Ridge. Not surprisingly, Canada, Greenland, and the US have also claimed that they should own this area of the Arctic Ocean because it is connected to their territories.

The Oil Industry

The Arctic environment

The Arctic Ocean is a harsh environment. It is so cold that part of it around the North Pole is permanently frozen, and large areas freeze each winter. In winter many months are permanently dark and there are thick sea fogs and strong winds. However, the waters are rich in wildlife. The nutrient-rich waters support large numbers of tiny algae, fed upon by plankton, which form an essential part of the food chain including larger fish, seabirds, and mammals such as seals and whales. The sea ice on the Arctic Ocean is also important for seals to give birth to their young and for polar bears to hunt on. Very few people live on the cold, treeless land edging the Arctic Ocean.

Oil impacts

For decades, oil has been drilled and produced from Arctic land, for example in Alaska, and also since the 1990s in shallow waters off Sakhalin Island, northeast Russia. There have been many impacts of the oil industry in the Arctic region already. For example, in 1989 an oil tanker called *Exxon Valdez* ran aground in Alaska and spilled 750,000 barrels of oil that killed hundreds of thousands of seabirds and polluted the coasts for decades.

< The supertanker *Exxon Valdez* caused huge concern worldwide in 1989 when it spilled oil in the pristine Alaskan Arctic waters.

Development fact

An Alaskan study estimated that development of the oil industry in US Arctic waters could create over 50,000 jobs and generate nearly $200 billion in government, state, and local revenue.

At Sakhalin, a Russian island in the North Pacific, millions of tons of oil industry waste were dumped at sea in a major salmon fishing area. Only large-scale international protests convinced oil companies to re-route subsea oil pipelines away from the feeding and breeding grounds of endangered grey whales.

Hazardous potential

Offshore drilling in the deep Arctic Ocean started in 2010 off Greenland and in 2011 Russian state-owned oil company Rosneft was planning to start a major drilling operation by 2015. BP was a possible production partner partly because of its experiences with the Gulf of Mexico spill in deep waters. Oil companies and environmentalists consider the freezing and rough Arctic Ocean conditions more hazardous than those of the Gulf of Mexico, with high potential for accidents and environmental damage. Therefore, companies such as Statoil are carrying out careful environmental reviews of possible drilling sites and plan to drill narrower than normal wells to slow the speed of oil production and reduce the chance of rapid oil loss from spills.

▽ **Walruses are Arctic mammals that are already threatened by loss of sea ice due to climate change. Pollution and disturbance by the oil industry could severely endanger them.**

The Oil Industry

Greenland waits

Russia, Canada, and the US want to exploit their offshore Arctic waters, and Lomonosov, for oil to help meet their populations' existing demand for oil. Greenland has little domestic demand for oil as its population is only around 57,000, but oil revenue is very important to the future development of the country. The country's main industries of fishing, some tourism, and gold mining provide insufficient money to run the country. It relies on financial help from Denmark, which partly controls Greenland. Greenlanders, who are mostly Inuit people, have only had legal rights to resources (minerals, as well as fish and whales) on and off their shores since 2009. Oil revenue from Greenland's Arctic Ocean sections and ideally Lomonosov would help it to become completely economically independent and to increase employment and the standard of living for its people.

▽ Arctic communities in Greenland and other countries would be transformed by oil development. But at what cost?

Destruction fact

Spilled oil and the toxic chemicals such as benzene that oil contains remain for longer in Arctic waters than in warmer seas. This is because bacteria break down oil more slowly in low temperatures.

Lomonosov Ridge, Arctic Ocean

The Inuit and other Arctic peoples, such as the Sami in northern Sweden and Dene in Canada, are trying to maximize oil revenue and minimize environmental damage, especially when it may affect their cultural traditions. For example, in 2010 Inuit people stopped Shell from drilling in Alaskan waters during periods when Bowhead whales visit coastal waters. This was to stop oil industry disturbance from scaring off the whales, partly because Bowhead hunting is an important part of Inuit culture.

Development or Destruction?

Development:

* Exploiting the oil reserves under the Lomonosov Ridge and other parts of the Arctic Ocean seafloor could increase global reserves by as much as one-tenth.
* Arctic oil could speed development and independence for Inuit and other Arctic peoples.
* Oil companies are exploring and producing Arctic oil slowly in order to lessen the chance of environmental damage.

Destruction:

* The Arctic is a unique habitat whose wildlife could suffer long-term damage by oil spills.
* The cold conditions of the Arctic region cause pollution to stay in the water for longer.
* The Arctic reserves are estimates and it could take decades before large amounts of oil are actually recovered.

Sustainable futures

Using oil is the very opposite of sustainable. It is a finite, nonrenewable natural resource that, once burned to release, disappears, leaving dwindling oil reserves for future generations. The pollution and greenhouse gases released through its production and use is harming the environment and causing climate change. So how can the oil industry and its development ever be sustainable?

Immediate oil futures

Many scientists believe that the world is past the point of its highest output of oil. Existing reserves may also not be as high as previously thought. In 2011 WikiLeaks published previously secret US documents that say Saudi Arabia's reserves may be 40 percent smaller than previously estimated. Global demand for oil is also increasing, especially in fast-growing economies with large populations, such as India and China. For example, there were just 250,000 private cars in China in the 1990s, but in 2010 alone around 7 million cars were sold. Uncertainty about oil supplies, made worse by political problems in oil-producing countries such as Libya, caused oil prices to reach their highest ever levels in 2011.

Chapter 7

ON THE SCENE

"If I were emperor of the world, I would put the pedal to the floor on energy efficiency and conservation for the next decade."

Stephen Chu, American physicist, 2007

Oil companies have only just started to find crude oil in the Arctic Ocean (see page 34) and have also started drilling off the Falkland Islands, near Antarctica, another potentially large source of crude oil. The tar sands and oil shale of countries such as Canada may contain 4 trillion barrels of oil and satisfy demand in the near future. However, extracting oil from these sources uses lots of energy, releases large amounts of greenhouse gases, and pollutes land and rivers used by indigenous peoples. This oil production could be made less damaging by using technology to reduce emissions and environmental pollution.

▽ **The Aptera hybrid car uses newly developed materials and technology to achieve fuel efficiency. It uses about 1 gallon per 330 miles (1 litre per 100 km).**

More efficient

If we are going to continue to use oil beyond the next few decades, then we are going to have to use it much more slowly. This can be achieved by extracting the maximum oil possible from reserves (see page 30) and by reducing spills, for example from old pipes (see page 23). It can also be achieved in many other ways, for example by using energy-efficient vehicles such as hybrid cars that use less fuel, using public transport, car sharing, and cycling.

The Oil Industry

Oil alternatives

Some people believe that remaining oil reserves should be left in the ground because of the threat from climate change and pollution caused by their extraction and use. The liquid fuels required by today's fleet of cars, airplanes, trains, and ships could, in theory, be supplied in part by biofuels. Biofuels include bioethanol made from crops such as corn or sugarcane, and biodiesel made from palm seed oil. They are renewable resources, and even though burning biofuel releases greenhouse gases, quantities are smaller than those released when burning oil. Crops also take in carbon dioxide as they grow.

EXPLORE FURTHER

Find out about the pros and cons of using different biofuels as oil replacements.

As growing crops use as much carbon when they grow as they release when they burn, they are considered carbon neutral. Biofuel crops are more sustainable than oil, but do cause environmental destruction, such as deforestation. Farmers cut down forests in some poorer parts of the world to create space for biofuels, because they can be a valuable export crop. This also means that they grow less food. In 2008 the World Bank calculated that increasing biofuel production caused three-quarters of worldwide price rises in foods.

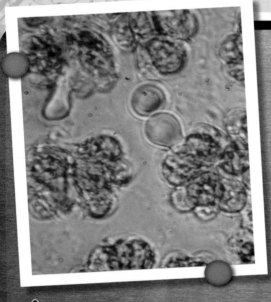

Innovations: Oil from algae

Around half of the weight of some types of green algae is oil. Scientists worldwide are developing ways to grow such algae in open ponds or clear plastic bags. The algae may be harvested and pressed to release oil or treated with chemicals to extract oil without killing the algae. Potentially, algae could yield over 24,000 gallons (90,000 liters) of biodiesel per hectare far more cheaply than crude oil.

△ In this microscopic view, it is possible to see the algae *Botryococcus* (green spheres) secreting bubbles of clear oil.

▲ Palm oil is sometimes called rainforest diesel because tropical forests are being destroyed to plant oil palms as biofuel crops.

A new world power?

A more sustainable alternative to oil and biofuel is to develop new renewable energy technologies that are virtually nonpolluting, have fewer land impacts, and create no greenhouse gases. The world has been in the age of oil through the twentieth and early twenty-first century, when oil fueled industrial growth, transportation, and other transformation. In the future the driving force could be hydrogen.

Hydrogen cells are special batteries that release energy to power vehicles using liquid hydrogen fuel. At present hydrogen power is little used, partly because it is expensive to make hydrogen fuel using electricity from fossil-fuel power stations. In the future, solar power might be used to create the fuel and there could be hydrogen filling stations in every town.

ON THE SCENE

"Ever since the car has been around we've been dependent on fossil fuels. What we need to do is to move on to electric power and in the long term, hydrogen. This is the seismic shift in terms of technologies underpinning how we power our cars."

Professor David Bailey, Coventry University Business School, UK

43

Debate club

Oil is discovered in the fields near a remote village. The people there have no electricity and most of them are subsistence farmers. Organize a debate to discuss drilling for oil in this village. You'll need six people to act as the characters below. They can use information from the book and the statements below to get started.

Each person should be given a chance to speak, without interruptions. Others in the class or group can listen to the speakers in the debate as if they are the developers. The developers have to decide at the end whose arguments are most convincing and why, and if they will proceed with the oil drilling.

STATE REPRESENTATIVE

"This region needs oil development and infrastructure because it will help raise the standard of living for people here to match that of people in other parts of the country."

TEENAGER

"I don't want to struggle in the fields for a living like my parents. I could get a job building wells or pipelines, maybe even training to get a better-paid job in the oil industry."

ENVIRONMENTALIST

"I have no doubt that drilling for and transporting oil will create spills and cause pollution. The soil and local rivers will never be the same again."

OLDER MAN

"Our family has farmed this land for centuries and I don't want things to change. I can't eat oil and I'm sure it will be the oil company who gets rich, not me."

OIL COMPANY REPRESENTATIVE

"We have lots of experience in getting oil out of the ground quickly and safely. Oil sales will benefit us all. Villagers can always find other farmland if need be."

LOCAL FACTORY OWNER

"I welcome the oil wells and local development. If there were new roads and power, I could make and transport goods more easily, employ more workers, and get richer!"

Glossary

algae Simple, plant-like organisms that grow in or near water. Seaweed is a type of algae.

bacteria Microscopic, single-celled organisms, some of which break down dead organisms and waste. Some kinds of bacteria can cause disease.

barrel Unit of measurement in the oil industry, equal to 42 gallons (191 liters).

blowout Sudden escape of oil from an oil well.

carbon footprint The direct effect someone's actions and lifestyle have on the environment in terms of carbon dioxide emissions.

climate change Changes in the world's weather patterns caused by human activity.

concession The right to use land or property for a specific purpose.

contamination When something is dirty or impure due to pollution or poison.

continental shelf Shallow area of underwater land surrounding a continent to a depth of approximately 600 feet (180 m).

crude oil Oil that has been extracted from the ground but not yet refined into a usable form.

deforestation Destroying or felling all the trees of a forest.

delta Area of land where a river splits into smaller rivers before entering the sea.

dugong Marine mammal that grazes on seagrass in warm, coastal waters.

emirate Territory ruled by a leader called an emir.

GDP Abbreviation for gross domestic product – the total value of goods and services produced by a country in one year.

geologist Scientist who studies the rocks and soil from which Earth is made.

greenhouse gas Gas in the upper atmosphere that warms the lower atmosphere around Earth by trapping the sun's heat.

hydraulic Describes machines operated by liquid moving under pressure.

infrastructure Facilities that serve a community such as roads and water and sewer systems.

Inuit People from northern Canada, parts of Greenland, and Alaska.

invest Spend money on something to make it better, more successful, or to make more money.

The Oil Industry

migrant Someone who moves from one place to live in another for a while.

nonrenewable Something that cannot be replaced once consumed, such as the energy resources oil and coal.

offshore In the sea, not far from land.

oil field Area overlying oil reserves with wells and/or rigs extracting oil.

onshore On land.

particle Very small piece of something.

petrochemical Chemical or product made from crude oil.

plankton Tiny organisms that float in the sea.

platform Large structure used for workers and machinery to drill wells in the seabed and extract oil.

refinery Factory that makes gas, diesel, and petrochemicals from oil.

reserve Oil that's still in the ground.

revenue Income, or money earned from a particular activity, such as oil production.

rig *See* platform.

riser Pipe carrying crude oil from reserve to surface.

sedimentary rock Type of rock formed by layers of sediment, such as sandstone.

sustainable Using natural resources to meet the needs of the present without jeopardizing those resources for future generations.

toxin Poison.

United Nations (UN) International organization promoting peace, security, and economic development.

World Bank Organization that lends funds to provide help to poorer member countries.

Web sites

Due to the changing nature of Internet links, Rosen Publishing has developed an online list of Web sites related to the subject of this book. This site is updated regularly. Please use this link to access the list:

http://www.rosenlinks.com/dod/oil

Index

The Oil Industry